SPEAKING *of* HENRY

Janet L. Meeks, M.A., LPCC, EdD

ISBN 979-8-88540-948-3 (paperback)
ISBN 979-8-88540-949-0 (digital)

Christian Faith Publishing
832 Park Avenue
Meadville, PA 16335
www.christianfaithpublishing.com

Printed in the United States of America

INTRODUCTION

While *Speaking of Henry* is fictional, it is inspired by the author's imagination of what her mother would be like as Mabel, Henry's big sister, in today's world. This manuscript is a continuation of Mabel's young life and her faith as she navigates personal, family, and friend struggles. It focuses on the lessons she learned from her deceased father and the lessons she is learning from her heavenly Father. While Mabel doesn't realize the impact her words and actions have on others, she is beginning to realize the impact others have on her. Mabel befriends a boy who others shun, and she helps her little brother see how very capable he is despite some serious academic challenges.

CHAPTER 1

Seasons Change

Fall was always my dad's favorite time of year. I think he just liked seeing Henry and me rake up all the leaves and jump into the colorful piles. Sometimes he would even join us if he didn't have too much yardwork to do! One thing was for certain though; Dad loved hearing us laugh, and he especially loved making us laugh.

Everything about fall reminded me of him. On the outside of the house, there was red, yellow, orange, and brown at every turn and the cool, crisp air that almost took my breath away each time I headed out the door. And on the inside, Mom's fall-scented candles filled every room, along with the smell of her pumpkin spice lattes. Even though fall was when my daddy left us and went to heaven, it was still my favorite season, too, because I could picture him in so many ways—playing in the leaves with us and dumping arms full of leaves on our heads, sitting at the kitchen counter, reading the newspaper, drinking one of Mom's lattes, and studying his Sunday school lesson in the swing on the back porch. Sometimes the picture in my mind was so clear, and then sometimes it was there, but it was fuzzy. I'm so afraid that someday, it will all be fuzzy. It's already that way for Henry. Sometimes I have to remind him of what Dad was like, and sometimes I even have to prove it by finding a picture. I don't want it to be that way for my little brother. I want him to always remember Dad, just the way I do. It makes me very sad to know that he doesn't.

"Get your jacket, Henry," I reminded him as I was heading out to the garage.

"You're not my mom!" he yelled back at me so that he got the last word. That's one thing about Henry I wish I could change. He always has to have the last word. That's gonna cause him problems someday; I just know it. I usually just ignore him. After all, if he gets cold, then I suppose he'll remember on his own tomorrow.

Mom was already in the car. She had honked the horn for us once and was getting ready to honk again when I opened the door. "What's taking so long? We're going to be late to school," Mom said, clearly a little aggravated.

"Well, Henry is trying to decide if he needs a jacket or not and if it would mean that I was right and he was wrong if he wore one and realized that he did, in fact, need it. He's also repeating in his head that I'm not his mother because I told him not to forget his jacket," I said in a snarky tone that I don't usually use.

Mom smiled at first but then quickly took a serious tone. "Now your brother is right about one thing. You're not his mother. You're his sister, and he needs you to be his sister."

Henry opened the car door in time to hear the last part and mumbled something under his breath. "All right, let's see if we can get this car out of the garage and get our attitudes in check," Mom said, trying to get the day started a little better than what it had.

It was another quiet ride to school. Mom turned on the radio, but I couldn't sing or hum along with Henry in the car. He had been very moody lately, I had noticed. Instead of asking him what was wrong, Mom and I just sort of ignored it, hoping it was just a phase and that it would pass.

Mr. Chapman was always there to greet us when we got out of the car. He said hello to Mom, and then he said, "Good morning, Mabel! Good morning, Henry!" as we came around in front of Mom's car. I responded, but Henry never even made eye contact; he just made a quick walk to the front doors of the school, like he was trying to avoid Mr. Chapman altogether.

Henry was inside before I was even halfway there. *Boy, he must really be mad at me,* I thought. *Was reminding him to get his jacket that big of a deal!*

The bell rang the moment I stepped into class. Thankfully, I didn't have to go to the office to get a tardy slip.

The school day was a typical one—writing, math, PE, lunch. That was my favorite half of the day. "When I grow up, I want to teach either writing, math, or PE...or maybe lunch," I chuckled to myself. Science and social studies were okay but just not my favorite.

As we were getting ready to start social studies, Mr. Foster, my fourth-grade teacher, lined us up for a bathroom break. I got in line beside Abigail and Storm. We couldn't talk while we were in line, but we still wanted to be in line together. As we got to the commons area, Storm, who was walking behind me, whispered in my ear, "Hey, isn't that your brother sitting in the hallway?"

I looked to the right of Abigail, and it sure was! Henry was sitting outside his teacher's door, his legs crisscrossed and his arms folded like he was mad.

What on earth is going on? I wondered. I tried to get his attention, but he had his head down and never looked up. I wanted to ask Mr. Foster if I could go check on him, but Mr. Foster was pretty strict, and I figured the answer would be no.

Later, when the first bell rang, I walked as fast as I could toward the front door. I wanted to talk to Henry before we got into the car. When he rounded the corner and got closer to me, I asked, "Hey, why were you sitting out in the hallway earlier?" I guess I did sound a little bit like a mother in that moment.

"What?" he asked like he didn't hear me.

"You heard me. Why were you sitting in the hallway? I saw you with your head down," I persisted.

Henry looked at me, still with a puzzled look on his face. Then, he appeared as though he had just realized what I was referring to. "Oh, that must've been when we were playing a game," he said as if it was no big deal.

"A game?" I questioned. "What kind of game?"

"You know. That switch-a-roo game where one person goes out into the hall, and everyone in the room gets up and moves seats. The teacher has one person hide in the back of the room. Then the person who was in the hallway comes in and tries to figure out who's missing," Henry explained rather quickly.

"What are you supposed to be learning from that?" I asked, thinking how that was a ridiculous waste of time.

"It's just a game, Mabel. You get to play games sometimes in first grade. We are kids, you know!"

"True," I admitted, but still, I didn't remember playing any game like that when I was in first grade. I was too busy learning to read and write.

The ride home was a little livelier than the ride to school. Mom was telling me that she bought some Girl Scout cookies—my favorite, the Do-si-Dos, and Henry's favorite, the Tagalongs. That made us both very happy! Then Henry started talking about that weird game his class played. I didn't really have anything exciting to tell other than Eddie getting sent to Mr. Chapman's office for popping his milk carton at lunch. That loud noise scared me to death! It must've scared the teachers, too, because they all came running out of the room where they eat their lunch.

"That's terrible," Mom said.

"I know. Eddie never came back to class. I don't know what happened to him," I added.

"Well, usually, the first time you go to the office, Mr. Chapman talks to you. And then if he thinks you listened, he gives you a piece of candy," Henry told as if he knew it as fact.

"Just how do you know that, John Henry Thompson?" Mom questioned.

"Uh, well that's just what Ralph told me. I really don't know," Henry corrected himself.

Something was off with Henry. I just knew it. He had been acting strangely, talking about things he shouldn't know anything about, and he just seemed like he wasn't being completely honest. I don't know what it is, but I do know that I'll find out because, after all, I *am* his sister.

CHAPTER 2

The Sleepover

I love Fridays, not because I get two days off from school—I love school!—but because, on Fridays, there's a good chance that I'll either get to sleep over at Storm's or she'll get to stay at my house. I think it's better for her to stay at my house because that gives her practice being away from home. Miss Jenny, her counselor, calls that "exposure therapy" or something of the sort. I've learned a lot from Storm about ways to self-calm and ways to talk to myself like I would talk to a friend. I've also learned to close my eyes and imagine I'm on the beach, feeling the heat of the sun, the breeze on my face and the cool water splashing onto my sandy toes. Of course, I can't think about that too much or it makes me want to take a nap, but it does come in handy right before a test.

This Friday was no different. Mom said Storm could come over, and I was so glad. We had plans to play in the leaves and clean up the treehouse. The last time Storm spent the night, we snuck some chocolate chip cookies up there, and we ended up with a bad case of ants. They were every-where! And if you've ever been in a confined area with a bunch of ants, you know that no matter how many showers you have afterward, you still feel like you have ants crawling all over your skin. It was awful! Anyway, I'm hoping the ants ate all the cookies and have found a new home.

"Last one in is a rotten egg!" my brother yelled as he darted out of the car and ran inside. It never gets old. Ordinarily, I would join right in, but I didn't want to appear childish in front of Storm. She doesn't have a little brother. She has an older brother who is already dating. Somehow, I find it hard to picture him yelling, "Last one in is a rotten egg!" Yeah, I think I'll just let it slide this time.

I helped Storm get her bag, and she grabbed her gym bag for dance lessons tomorrow. I've always wanted to dance, but my body just isn't having it. Storm makes it look so easy with her leotard, tutu, and ballet slippers. She's just so…so graceful. My middle name is Grace, but it's definitely not short for graceful!

We made our way to the door, and as soon as we entered the house, Henry was right there to call me the rotten egg. "Ha ha! You're last! That makes you the rotten egg!" he laughed, pointing right at me.

"Come on, Storm," I said. "Let's go to my room."

Henry didn't seem to care that I ignored him. He followed us all the way to my bedroom, saying that I was the rotten egg, probably because I usually won that little game. This was his celebratory moment, so I suppose I shouldn't spoil it for him.

"That's right, Henry. You got me," I said, trying my best to let him feel like he had the upper hand. "You won. You beat me. What can I say?" I went on and on.

Henry stopped and just looked at me. All at once, he waved at me and ran off. What a funny little guy, annoying sometimes, but I just love him all the same. I sorta think he has a bit of a crush on Storm because it's like he tries to flirt with her, but he doesn't know how. Like on the car ride home, he asked, "So how long are you going to get to stay, Storm?" She told him she had to leave early Saturday morning because she has dance lessons on Saturdays. Then he said, "Oh, that's too bad. I was thinking of going to the movies on Saturday." Now just what does that mean! It's not like he can drive yet! Mom smiled when he said it. I just raised my eyebrows high on my forehead with my mouth gaping open, and Storm actually blushed a little, I think. It was cute and sounded so much older than what he is. And then he had to go play the "last one in is a rotten egg" card. Hilarious!

We got settled and dumped all of our stuff in my room. Storm was looking at some old jewelry Mom had given me. There was one bracelet that she kept looking at. It had some brown and green rock thingies on it. She seemed to really like it, so I asked her if she wanted it. She said, "No, I couldn't."

I said, "Yes, you can. Mom gave me a bunch of her old jewelry. I'm sure she wouldn't care if I gave you one. Mommm!" I yelled, just so I could double-check.

"Yes, Mabel, you don't have to yell. I'm right here."

"I'm sorry. I just wanted to see if it was okay for me to give this bracelet to Storm."

Mom looked over at Storm who was still admiring the bracelet. "Of course. I've had that bracelet for a long time. A friend of mine gave it to me a very long time ago, but I just really never had anything I could wear with it. I think he would be happy that it gets some wear," Mom said as she fastened the bracelet around Storm's hand. "That looks really good on you, Storm."

"Whoa, whoa, wait just a minute! Did you say 'he' would be happy?" I asked, unsure of what "he" she was meaning.

"An old friend from college, Mabel. That's all," Mom said with a mysterious look on her face.

I thought for a minute and then asked a question that had entered my mind a time or two before. "Mom, do you think you'll marry someone other than Dad?" I asked, not sure I wanted to hear the answer.

"Well, Mabel, I'm not planning on it, but I suppose God would be the only person who knows the answer to that question."

I thought for a second and wondered if that answer could be found in my little pink book. I'll have to check that out because Daddy said that I could find all the answers in that book. Since I didn't respond right away, Mom made a quick escape for the kitchen and got started making dinner.

"Thanks for the bracelet, Mabel! I don't have any jewelry other than a ring my mom gave me on my birthday."

"It does look really good on you! I'm glad you like it! Now come on, let's go check out the tree house and see if the ants have found a new home."

We went downstairs and tried to grab some snacks, but Mom reminded me that dinner would be ready soon. As we opened the back door, Henry asked if he could come too. I told him he could if he would make a new sign. The rain ruined the last one, so I told him to get a small, white poster board out of the office and to write "Do Not Trespass."

Henry said, "Okay, I'll make a sign and put it where the old one was. Then I'll come up, okay?"

"Okay," I agreed.

Storm and I started up the wooden steps that were nailed into the side of the tree. When we got to the top, it was clear that the ants had *not* found a new home. We tried to shoo them away, but did you know that you can't shoo an ant? So we took off our tennis shoes and started trying to get rid of them once and for all. Just when we thought we had a handle on the situation, Henry showed up with a deck of cards in his hand. We played a few hands of Crazy Eights and talked about everything you can imagine. Then Mom called me to set the table.

We climbed down the tree one at a time. Henry and Storm had started toward the back door by the time I reached the bottom. I was about to holler and tell them to wait up when I spotted something that made me stop right in my tracks. It was the sign—the sign I had asked Henry to make—only there was something seriously wrong. Instead of it saying "Do Not Trespass," it said "adtensspsct." It was all jumbled up, and no one, including me, would be able to read it! I didn't expect him to spell it perfectly, but I didn't even know what that was! Something was definitely going on with him.

We finished dinner and then headed to the basement and found a movie that we all agreed on. I really didn't want Henry barging in on my company, but there was no way I was going to ignore him or tell him to leave us alone. Henry needs me, I thought. *And I'm always gonna be there for him.*

CHAPTER 3

Here We Go Again

I didn't mention the sign to Henry. I sorta talked myself out of it. So what if he isn't a writer like me? Maybe he's good at math or science or social studies. We're all good at different things, right? Or maybe, knowing Henry, he was just being silly or was mad because I told him he couldn't come up to the tree house until he made the sign. Yeah, that was it. That's why he made such a ridiculous sign. He wanted me to see it! He wanted me to say something! He's such a stinker sometimes.

Henry doesn't let me walk him to class anymore. I suppose it had to end sometime, but I really thought it would be a while longer. When I got to class, Mr. Foster already had a math worksheet on our desks. It was so easy, I finished it before the bell rang. Unfortunately, all we can do when we finish is read a book. I used to love it when Mrs. Lamkey started the day with writing because I could spend the *whole* day doing that. Anyway, at least it was a free day at PE, and I was sure happy about that!

As we left the gym, Mr. Foster took us to the commons area and let us get a drink and use the restroom if we needed to. When I came out of the restroom, I saw Henry. He was sitting outside his classroom door again, his legs crisscrossed and his head down. Were they playing that ridiculous game again? Surely not. I was getting ready to ask Mr. Foster if I could go check on my brother when I saw Mr. Chapman coming out of his office. He didn't look happy. He didn't look happy at all. And then it happened. He was actually headed to see my little brother. He stood tall, looking down at Henry, his hands on his hips and his voice stern. I couldn't hear all of it, but it was clear to me that Henry was in trouble. Mr. Chapman reached out his hand, Henry took it, and Mr. Chapman helped him to his feet. The two walked toward the office with Mr. Chapman talking the whole way and Henry looking down at his feet.

I asked Mr. Foster if I could go make sure my brother wasn't sick because I had seen him go to the office. Mr. Foster said, "Sure, just be quick." That was all I needed. I raced to the office as fast as I could walk without running. When I went into the office, Mrs. Rose, the school secretary, said, "Well, hello, Mabel? How are you today?"

"I'm doing just fine, Mrs. Rose. How are you today?" I asked, making sure I used all of my manners.

"I'm having a wonderful day," she replied.

"Well, I was having a pretty wonderful day, too, until I saw Henry. Is he in there?" I asked as I pointed toward Mr. Chapman's office.

"I'm afraid he is, dear," Mrs. Rose said with a sad glance toward the door.

"Was he playing that game?" I asked.

"What game?" she questioned, looking very confused.

"Never mind. Well, is he sick?"

"No, he's not sick," she said, reluctant to give me any details.

"Well, what's wrong with him?" I asked. I was starting to get really worried about Henry and about the fact that Mr. Foster told me to make it quick.

"I don't know, Mabel, but he'll be all right with Mr. Chapman."

I don't know what happened to me at that moment, but I marched straight past Mrs. Rose's desk and knocked on Mr. Chapman's door. I didn't wait for him to open the door; I just opened it right up before Mrs. Rose could tell me to stop. "Why are you in the principal's office?" I asked Henry.

"You're not my—" he started.

"Don't even go there, Henry! I know I'm not your mother, okay, but I *am* your sister, and I *am* worried about you! What is going on?" I demanded.

He sat there in silence with his head down now. The side of his face was red, and I couldn't quite tell if he was mad or sad or just being bad.

"Henry, if you don't tell me what's wrong, I *am* going to tell your mother when she picks us up today," I threatened, hoping he would say something, but Mr. Chapman interrupted.

"There's no need to tell your mother, Mabel," Mr. Chapman said. "Henry has promised he will change his ways."

At that moment, Roger came to the door and told me that Mr. Foster said to hurry up. "Henry, you and I are going to have a little talk when we get home, do you hear me?" Okay, I'll admit, that really did sound like Mom, but he didn't respond at all.

I hurried back to class, but again, my mind was preoccupied with Henry. He and I were definitely going to have a talk, but I'd have to somehow tone it down and not sound like a mom, or he would just shut down again. I went over it in my head a hundred times during the rest of the day. That means I didn't hear a word about science or social studies.

I looked at Henry when I got to the pickup line and gave him every opportunity to come clean before we got into the car—nothing, I got nothing. As Mom pulled up, he grabbed the string on my backpack and pulled me back just a bit. "Please don't say anything to Mom," Henry pleaded. He did look somewhat remorseful, but I didn't cut him any slack.

"We're gonna talk when we get home, Henry, and you're gonna tell me what's going on," I said with authority.

"Okay, I will. I promise. Just please don't say anything. You promise?"

"I promise," I said after I exhaled loudly and rolled my eyes at him. I got into the car and closed the door. He did the same. Mom kept trying to ask about our day, but that's about as far as the conversation went. He looked at me and shook his head no, pleading still. I kept my mouth shut, at least for the moment.

As soon as we got home and dropped our book bags, I took ahold of Henry's shirt and pulled him toward the stairs. I let go of his shirt and then motioned with my finger for him to follow me.

I went into my room, and Henry followed and closed the door behind him. "Okay, fess up," I insisted. "Stop looking at your feet and tell me what's wrong, Henry." I have to admit; I was losing my patience. I feel responsible for Henry. I know I'm not his parent, but I do have to look after him.

That's why I always walked him to class. I have to be sure that he's okay.

"All right, I was just humming in class, and Mrs. Jones had asked me to stop several times. I don't know. I just got this tune in my head, and I couldn't get it out. So I was humming," he admitted.

"You got sent to the office because you were humming?" I asked, trying to figure this situation out the best I could.

"Yes, that's exactly what happened. I was humming, and she just sent me out in the hallway. And then, Mr. Chapman showed up, and he wasn't very happy to see me there," Henry explained, although I couldn't help thinking there was a little more to the story than that.

"Henry, you're gonna get in big trouble if you get sent to the office again! I mean it!" I scolded.

"I won't do it again. I promise. Please just don't say anything to Mom." He was almost crying at this point.

I explained to Henry that we all make mistakes and that he has now made his. I told him that I wanted good things for him and that he had to pay attention in class so that he could learn. I tried really hard not to sound like a mom, but I just failed miserably. He took it well though, and he hugged me like he's never hugged me before. "Thanks, sissy," he said and I could tell that he was trying not to cry.

Being a parent can't be easy because being a big sister is hard work! I thought to myself. The hug at the end, though, made it all seem okay.

CHAPTER 4

The Donkey or the Ox

The next morning, I heard Mom in Henry's room talking to him. *Did he come clean with her?* I wondered. "Did he tell her that he had to go to Mr. Chapman's office? She's gonna kill him! Well, maybe not kill him, but he's definitely not going to see the light of day for a long while. He'll be grounded until he gets to fourth grade!" I worried.

I put my ear up to the wall to see if I could hear what was going on, but I couldn't. Suddenly, Mom entered my room. "Mabel, what on earth are you doing?" she asked, knowing full well I was trying to hear them.

"What's wrong with Henry?" I asked, trying to get her to forget what she had just seen.

"He's not feeling well today," she explained. "He says his belly hurts."

I looked away and acted like it was no big deal, but this was just one more strange thing with Henry. I don't think he was sick. I don't think he was sick at all, but I promised Henry I wouldn't say anything to Mom. "Well, I'll be down in a few minutes," I told Mom.

"Okay. I'll have breakfast on the table. Do you want milk or orange juice?"

"Orange juice will be just fine," I replied.

After Mom made her way downstairs, I tiptoed over to Henry's bedroom and opened the door to find him playing a handheld video game. "What are you doing, Henry?" I asked, already frustrated with his lying.

He slid back underneath the covers and laid the video game aside. "I'm not feeling very well. My throat hurts," he blurted out.

"I thought your belly hurt?"

"Well, it hurts too—my throat and my belly," Henry said. He did look a little pale. But knowing him, he probably looked up "how to make yourself look pale" on the internet and did just that.

I thought for a minute about what to say next, but instead, I just hurried to get ready. "Have a good day, Henry. I hope you feel better soon!" I said sarcastically.

I forgot until morning announcements that it was report card day. I was excited to get mine because I know, in fourth grade, you get to be on the honor roll if you have all As and Bs. I definitely wanted to be on that! I wanted my name to be in the paper, and I wanted to be able to tell my whole family that I was on the honor roll. Mr. Foster talked about it all day long and made us wait until the last ten minutes of class before he gave us our report cards. I was starting to get really nervous, and my palms started getting all sweaty. I had to remind myself to breathe slowly through my nose and out through my mouth. Miss Jenny was sure a smart lady, because that worked like a charm.

Finally, Mr. Foster called my name. I walked up to his desk, and he told me I should've done better; then he winked. I waited until I got back to my seat to open it. Then I slowly opened the white folded paper—math, A; science, A-; reading, A+; writing, A+; social studies, A-; PE, A; music, A. "Oh my gosh! I got all As? I got all As!" I screamed silently. "Mom is going to be so proud of me!" I looked around at my friends, and they seemed pretty pleased with their report cards as well. I didn't have time to ask them what they got because Mrs. Jones appeared at the door and asked Mr. Foster if she could see me for a minute. I got up and went to the door. "Hi, Mrs. Jones," I said, unsure of what she wanted with me.

"Hello, Mabel, would you mind to give this to your mother? Henry was absent today, and I wanted to be sure and get this to her."

"Sure! I'd be happy to," I replied. Mrs. Jones handed me a manila envelope and thanked me. I turned around and headed back to my seat.

The manila envelope wasn't sealed. It just had the clip fastened at the top. I could look at Henry's report card, and no one would ever know. I wondered how he did. I knew he didn't make all As because, in first grade, you only get S for satisfactory, P for progressing, NI for needs improvement, or U for unsatisfactory. I was trying to picture Henry in class. Did he participate? Did he get his work posted? Did he get smiley faces on his work? I looked up toward the front of the room for a minute, but I couldn't wait any longer. I had to know. I slowly unfastened the gold-colored clasp and carefully pulled his report card out. The front said "John Henry Thompson" and "First Grade" on it. I opened it up and started down the left side. I couldn't believe my eyes. Henry had NI and U on everything! On the right side of the report card were "Behavior," "Work Ethic," and "Responsibility." Henry had a U on all three of these with a note from Mrs.

Jones, requesting a conference! What on earth was happening! How could I be so happy with my report card when Henry was clearly in trouble? I folded the card back up and slid it back into the envelope, sealing it again with the clasp.

The bell rang, and out the door I went. I didn't even say goodbye to my friends. All I could think about was that I had to get home to Henry. I had to hear his explanation. Should I tell Mom, or do I keep my promise? It all seemed very muddy right now, and to be honest, I had no idea what I was going to do.

I was in the pickup line, waiting for Mom to pull up. She finally made it to where I was standing, and I noticed Henry in the back seat. I got into the car and turned to look at Henry. "Feeling better?" I asked.

"No, not really. I went to the doctor today," he said.

"Yes, the doctor said there was a stomach bug going around. A lot of people have it right now, so don't get close to Henry and remember to wash your hands a lot when you're at school," Mom instructed.

"Mom, I'm in a car with him, two feet away. If he has a stomach bug, I'm pretty sure we're all gonna have it."

"Well, just do the best you can. We're going straight home," Mom said.

Another quiet ride home, and I jumped out of the car as soon as Mom put it in park. I grabbed my book bag and left Henry behind. I kicked my shoes off and ran upstairs, locking the door behind me. I went over to my desk, sat down, and pulled out the pink book my father had given me. I knew the answer would be in there because I struggled to know what to do. I think there's something wrong, and I think Henry is acting up in class so he won't be embarrassed, and I think it's only gonna get worse until an adult can intervene. This is too much for me to take care of. After all, as Henry reminds me quite frequently, I'm not his mother.

I opened the book and read a little bit. Nothing was really sounding like what I was dealing with. I searched for a little while longer, and then I just stopped and prayed. I prayed and asked what to do to help my little brother. I prayed for help in knowing how to talk to him like a sister, not a mother. And I prayed that Jesus would tell my daddy I said hello and that I love him and miss him so very much. And then I said, "Amen."

Instantly, and I mean instantly, I felt better. I remembered that I am never alone and that I am strong. I remembered, in that moment, something that my dad always told me. He told me to "always do what is right, not what is easy." It wasn't easy to break a promise to my little brother. It wasn't easy to show a spectacular report card, knowing that my brother's was just the opposite. And it wasn't easy to understand what was going on, but I just knew something was.

I remembered something else too, something my Sunday school teacher said she did sometimes. Mrs. Angie told us that whenever she had trouble finding what she was looking for in the Bible that sometimes she just flipped through it and stopped on a certain page. If it worked for her, it's gotta work for me. I picked up my pink Bible and flipped through the pages from the very back to the very front, stopping on a random page. I put the book down on my desk, closed my eyes, and just ran my finger down the page, stopping at one point, just above the bottom of the book. When I opened my eyes, I read Deuteronomy 22:4 (NIV), "If you see your fellow Israelite's donkey or ox fallen on the road, do not ignore it. Help the owner get it to its feet."

I thought for a minute, and then I realized that Henry needed help. I couldn't ignore it any longer; I *had* to help him get back on his feet. I knew exactly what I needed to do in that moment; I had to tell Mom. I waited for Henry to go to bed; his bedtime was an hour earlier than mine. We played a game together after Mom cleaned up the dinner dishes. I paid close attention to Henry and noticed something that had happened so many times before; it just stood out to me this time. Every time Henry had to draw a card, he handed it to me or Mom to read. Why wasn't he trying? Even if he couldn't read some of the words, he never even tried. Mom eventually won the game, and Henry got to stay up a little longer than normal. As soon as he made his way to his bedroom and shut the door, I tried to think of how to approach the subject.

Mom was talking about school and Mr. Chapman and saying what a nice principal Mr. Chapman was. I continued to think about the best way to bring Henry up, but it seemed like all she wanted to talk about was my principal. She finally mentioned that Henry really wanted to win the game tonight and how she felt badly about winning. At that, I jumped in and said, "Speaking of Henry…"

"Yes," Mom said.

"Have you ever noticed that he doesn't read any of the cards when we play Sorry! or Monopoly or any other game?" I asked, hoping she would recognize there was a problem.

"Yes, honey, but he's only six."

"I know, but I think he should at least be trying to sound out words. Have you ever seen his writing?" I continued.

"Well, not a lot. I just thought he was getting his homework done at school," Mom said, now paying a little more attention to what I was saying.

"Look at this sign he made, Mom." I reached under the cushion on the couch where I had stashed his sign and his report card, and I held up the sign.

"What does that say?" she asked, clearly confused.

"It says 'Do Not Trespass.' I asked him to make a sign for the tree house. And I'm really worried, Mom. I've seen him in trouble twice at school, but he lied about it the first time. And then he got sent to the principal's office a second time. And look, Mom." I pulled out his report card and placed it in her hands. She opened it, and her mouth fell open.

"Mabel, why didn't you…" she started, and then she stopped herself.

"I know, Mom, I'm sorry. I'm so very sorry. It has all happened so fast, and then I started noticing things that just seemed a little off. I'm so worried, Mom. What are we gonna do?"

"Well, you, my dear, are going to go to bed so that you'll be ready for school tomorrow. Thank you so much for telling me. I appreciate you looking after your little brother the way that you do. You know he loves you, right?" she said, trying to reassure me.

"Yes, and I love him. Please don't tell him that I told you all of this. I promised him that I wouldn't tell."

"It'll be okay, Mabel. Everything is going to be okay."

"I love you, Mom," I said with that stupid lump thing in my throat again. I hugged Mom and headed upstairs. When I turned to look back at Mom, I found exactly what I thought I'd find—her hands clenched, her head bowed, and her eyes closed, praying. I think I'll go do the same.

CHAPTER 5

The Meeting

Mom woke us up earlier than normal. I could smell French toast and figured she just wanted us to have a good breakfast before school. I *love* French toast, so I wasted no time getting dressed and ready for school. By the time I got to the kitchen, Henry was already getting some more milk. Clearly, he loves French toast too because his plate was already empty, except for a little bit of syrup and what was still around his mouth.

Mom acted like her normal self. She was smiling, asking us how we liked our breakfast. Did she and I have a conversation about Henry last night, or was that just a dream? I wasn't certain because she wasn't acting like she knew Henry got only NI and U on his report card. Most moms would have been upset. Most moms would have grounded one kid for misbehaving and the other for not telling her sooner. Most moms would still be mad come morning. But not my mom. My mom was thoughtful about everything she said. She took her time to mull things over and pray about them. She was always careful not to hurt anyone's feelings. And she was simply a really nice mom, not just to her kids but to everybody. And she was pretty too to be so old—thirty-six, I think.

I handed Henry a damp paper towel and motioned that he had something on his mouth. I could tell he was starting to tell me that I wasn't his mom again, but when I raised my eyebrows in a "I dare you" kind of way, he stopped himself and wiped his mouth, like I had instructed.

Mom asked about it being time for report cards as we headed down the road. *Yep, now I know that conversation took place,* I thought to myself. I was sure hoping she didn't let Henry know that I had broken my promise to him.

I jumped in to respond. "Uh, yes, I need you to sign mine, Mom. I'll get it out and have it ready. Do you have a pen?" I asked, trying not to sound like I did really well or really badly either.

"I've got a pen. So how did you do?" she asked.

I wanted to scream that I made all As and that my name was gonna be in the newspaper. I wanted to ask if I could call Uncle Rick tonight and tell him and Aunt Deb. But I also didn't want to brag, especially in front of Henry, so I just said, "I did fine. I was happy with it." Even that felt wrong as I imagined how Henry was gonna feel when he laid eyes on his report card.

"Henry, what about you? Did you get your report card?" Mom asked in a nonchalant way.

"I've been home sick, remember?" he said, giving himself a little bit of an out.

"That's right. You've been home with a bellyache."

"And a sore throat," Henry quickly added.

Mom drove down the street toward the school, but she missed the turn to go to the drop-off line. "Where are we going?" Henry asked with a panic in his voice.

"Well, I want to go in and get your report card, Henry. I need to know how both of my kids are doing in school," she said.

Mom is also very smooth. That was the smoothest move I've ever seen from her or dad. She wasn't going to let Henry know that I ratted on him. Whew! I was so glad about that!

She pulled into a parking spot and reached for an ink pen in her purse. I handed her my report card. She opened it up, and her eyes lit up. "Mabel, you got—"

"I did just fine, Mom. I was happy with it," I interrupted her.

Mom looked in the rearview mirror at me, and I gave her a glance that let her know I didn't want her to brag about me in front of Henry. She picked up on it quickly, I think, because she said, "Well, we will talk about this more tonight."

I looked over at Henry and could tell he was wondering if I had something not too great on my report card because he couldn't tell from what Mom was saying if I did great or not so great.

"Okay," I said as I took my report card back and shoved it into my backpack.

We all walked into the building together. As we headed down the long hallway, Mom dropped me off at Mr. Foster's class. "Bye, Mom! Bye, Henry!" Henry really did look sick now. His face was red, his eyes looked teary, and he looked like he was sweating even though it was really cool this morning.

I stood at my classroom door and watched Mom and Henry walk down the hallway, Mom still talking to Henry like nothing was wrong. And then they disappeared around the corner. I worried about my little brother off and on all day. I didn't see him in the hallway, and we have different lunch schedules, so I had to wait until the first bell rang to see him again.

I was so glad he wasn't mad at me. He seemed to have forgotten that Mom came to school with him. He didn't talk about his report card at all. He was looking forward to getting home and playing his video games. *What's going on? I wondered. Isn't he in trouble? Didn't Mom sign his report card? Didn't she talk to Mrs. Jones? Is she gonna talk to him tonight?* All these questions were swimming in my head as Henry was laughing with his friend and acting like his world was perfect.

The ride home was no different. Mom acted like everything was fine. Henry was just being silly. And I'm more confused now than ever! I kept trying to catch Mom's eye when she looked in her mirror, but she kept her eyes on the road the whole way home, not once glancing back at me. Maybe she didn't have the meeting after all. Maybe Henry had a sub today. *I don't understand adults at all. They are just the weirdest humans on the planet!* I thought to myself.

Mom opened the garage, pulled in, and as soon as she shut the engine off, Henry hopped out of the car and raced inside to his video games. I looked at mom and said, "Okay, what's the deal? What did Mrs. Jones say? Why is Henry in such a good mood and not grounded until he's ten?" I demanded to know.

Mom stepped out of the car. I thought she was ignoring me until I stepped out of the car too. She stood a foot from me and faced me. "First of all, Mabel, I want you to know how very proud I am of you. I know you are super excited about your report card and having all As—"

"But—" I tried to interject, but Mom wasn't having it.

"No, I want you to know that you can be happy about your report card. You *should* be happy, Mabel. You worked really hard on that. So I am very proud of you! And, yes, we are calling Uncle Rick and Aunt Deb tonight so you can tell them the good news," Mom said, smiling.

"But what about Henry?"

Mom's face turned from a smile to worry. "I met with Henry's teacher and with Mr. Chapman. They think Henry has something wrong with how he sees his letters and numbers. I'm going to need to take him to a special doctor to have some tests done to be sure," she explained. "And they think that Henry is acting out in class because he's embarrassed that he can't read and write and do math as well as his classmates. He's really struggling, Mabel, but we are going to get him help. I've already called, and I was able to get him into the doctor next week. I'm going to talk to him tonight to explain everything to him the best way I can."

"Do you need me to help?" I offered.

"No, Mabel, I just need you to be the best big sister you can be," she said.

"I can do that," I reassured Mom.

"I know you can," she replied. "Now let's go make a phone call! Last one in is a rotten egg," Mom laughed.

She's the best mom in the whole wide world! I thought to myself. *The absolute best.*

CHAPTER 6

Eddie

It was my Friday to spend the night at Storm's house. While I didn't want to leave Mom and Henry, I didn't want to disappoint Storm either. After all, she was such a good friend! I knew all of her secrets and she knew mine...well, except for the Henry thing. But I'll probably tell her all about that tonight.

I had my favorite green plaid bag packed and ready to take with me to school. Storm was supposed to wait for me inside the front door. Sure enough, I could see her waving when Mom pulled up. I was really excited to see her. In fact, I was so excited, I almost missed the rather strange interaction between Mr. Chapman and my mother. Mom wound down the window to say hello to him. Mr. Chapman walked over to the car, completely forgetting to say hi to me or to Henry, and he said, "Good morning, Maggie."

Maggie! What is that all about? What happened to "Good morning, Mrs. Thompson?" I turned around to look as I headed toward the door, and Mr. Chapman was holding up the drop-off line. There were several cars behind Mom, and I was certain they all had places to go and people to see. Then I saw Mom move her blonde curly hair out of her eyes. *Was the sun in her eyes? It was actually a little cloudy this morning,* I thought to myself. This was really odd. Only Mom's friends call her Maggie. Was Mr. Chapman Mom's friend? That's a silly thought. He's my principal; he can't be Mom's friend. As soon as I got inside, Storm started telling me about our sub for the day, and I forgot all about what I had just seen and heard.

Our substitute teacher today was only ten years older than we were. She looked like a big sister, not a teacher. Her name was Miss Thomas. She was short, and tiny. I'm telling you, I think I could win if we wrestled in the floor. Her ears were triple pierced, her black hair long and wavy, and she had on the cutest blue and tan sweater with three necklaces, *and* she was wearing jeans! She reminded me of my cousin, Carley, who's away at college, except Carley doesn't wear as much jewelry, and she doesn't have black hair. Miss Thomas was full of energy, which was good because you definitely need a lot of energy to take care of my class, especially with Eddie. I don't know why he's so mean, but he's mean. I just try to stay away from him, and that usually works. Well, it worked until today.

Miss Thomas called me to the front of the room and turned around with her back to the class so that no one could hear what she said. "Mabel, Mr. Foster left me a note, saying that I might want to see if it would be okay with you if I put Eddie beside you in class and at lunch. Would that be okay?"

"Uh," I said, trying to think of what my response should be. "I guess so," I mumbled, not knowing why I said that. It just sorta slipped right off my tongue.

"I really appreciate it. Mr. Foster said you would be the best influence on Eddie and that it's sometimes hard to keep him calm," Miss Thomas explained.

I found my way back to my seat, and Miss Thomas waited a few minutes and then asked, "Mabel, would you mind to change seats with Michael?"

Wait just a minute! What's happening? I was so confused. I thought Miss Thomas wanted to move Eddie closer to me and my friends. I must've misunderstood because what she really meant was that she was moving me over in front of Eddie. Just like a robot, I picked up my books and walked slowly over to the seat in front of Eddie. Michael was still collecting his belongings, so I just stood there. I glanced behind Michael and looked at Eddie. He was sitting there quietly, using his number 2 pencil to carve out a hole into his desk. He had already drawn a quite elaborate picture on his desk—fire-breathing dragons, and swords, and people in armor. Wow, he was really quite talented. All of a sudden, he stopped carving and looked up at me with a wild look in his eyes, like a coyote or some other wild animal straight out of the woods. He was cute in a strange sort of way. He had short, blonde hair, but it was pretty curly. His eyes were blue, crystal blue almost, like you could see an ocean in there if you looked hard enough. His skin was pale, and he had a pretty good-sized scar on the left side of his face. His jeans had holes in them, but I don't think he bought them that way. And he had grass stains all over his clothes and a little bit of what appeared to be dirt on his elbows.

"What are you staring at!" he growled. I mean that; he really did growl.

"Nothing, Eddie. How are you today?" I asked like I hadn't just heard a growl from a nine-year-old boy.

He didn't respond. He just went back to carving a hole in his desk. Miss Thomas walked over to see what was taking Michael so long when she saw the drawings and the hole on

Eddie's desk. "Eddie, get a paper towel and some cleaner and wipe your desk off!" Miss Thomas demanded.

I knew Eddie, and I knew that it didn't take much to send him over the edge. Quickly, I looked at Miss Thomas and asked, "Would it be okay if we just waited until the end of the day? I mean, it might help Eddie if he can see his drawings. It's Friday anyway. We can clean it at the end of the day." I looked at Miss Thomas and nodded my head yes, as if I was telling her she needed to agree with me. It worked. She agreed, and Michael moved to my seat beside Storm, Abigail, Jenny, and Roger. And here I was, in front of the meanest boy in the whole school. *Great, jusstt grrreat!*

We were about ten minutes into math class when Eddie started writing on my back. It felt like he was working the math problems across my shoulders, but he was acting like he was using an ink pen and then a marker. He made sure that I saw both. I kept pulling the top part of my shirt over my shoulder to see if I could see his markings, but I couldn't see anything. I asked him nicely to please stop, but the niceness was wearing off fast.

"Stop it!" I demanded. He just smirked and didn't say anything back. I scooted up as far as I could in my seat, and that seemed to help, at least for a little bit. Then he started putting his feet underneath my desk and kicked constantly. I couldn't hear anything Miss Thomas was teaching because Eddie eventually maneuvered his feet to somehow lift my desk. He was so strong to be so skinny! He did that about ten times, and I was starting to feel like I was on a ride at the amusement park.

I glanced across the room at Storm, and she mouthed, "I'm so sorry." I just shook my head and tried my best to pay attention.

I eventually got tired of sitting like I was, and I leaned back in my chair. At that point, Eddie started blowing on the back of my neck. Then he put something wet on my neck. I don't even wanna know what that was! I just pulled the neck of my shirt up and tried desperately to wipe the wetness off, acting like it didn't bother me. But it most certainly did bother me. It was gross! So gross! I wondered why Eddie was like that. I wondered what made that awful place on his face. I wondered what his mom and dad were like. I wondered if he had any brothers or sisters and if they were just like him.

Eddie kept bothering me until it was time for lunch. He sang songs, hummed, tapped his pencil—you name it, he did it. It was like he was trying to get a reaction from me. I kept reminding myself of something my dad always told me. He would say, "Mabel, there's good in everybody. You just have to look a little harder in some than others." Well, I don't think Dad ever met Eddie, but I was still gonna give Eddie a chance.

We lined up for lunch. And as we headed out of the classroom, Eddie, who was still right behind me, stepped on the back of my right shoe. I almost fell onto Jonah who was standing in front of me. I ignored Eddie and didn't even turn around. Then he did it again…and again…and again. Finally, I had to stop and put my shoes back on because they both had come completely off my feet. That was it! I'd had enough!

I ran to catch up and got back in line. I took four or five steps and turned around just as Eddie was getting ready to step on my shoes again, and I looked him right in the eyes and said, "Eddie, you know, you'd have a lot of friends if you were just a little bit nicer. I'd like you. My friends would like you, and if you had friends, you wouldn't have to act like this. You could laugh and have fun and have people to play with at recess instead of having to stand against the wall for all the trouble you caused in class. Do you hear me, Eddie! Do you hear what I'm saying?" I was preaching pretty good by the time we got to lunch. Eddie didn't respond at all. He looked stunned. He looked…he looked…well he just looked stunned. He ate lunch in silence. He didn't mix his foods together or throw anything or pop his milk carton. He acted like a normal kid. I tried to say something to him, but I couldn't think of anything and, to be quite honest, I was pretty tired after dealing with him all morning.

The true test would come on our walk back to class. Believe it or not, Eddie didn't step on my feet a single time. In fact, when we got back to the room, he picked up the cleaner, grabbed a paper towel, and headed over to his desk.

"Wait, Eddie! I told Miss Thomas we would clean it at the end of the day. Don't clean it now. It's *really* good! I wish I could draw like that!" I said, even though I would never draw dragons and fire and scary stuff. Still his artwork was spectacular.

Again, Eddie looked at me, stunned. He put down the cleaner and said, "Why are you being so nice to me?"

I had never seen Eddie so calm. He wasn't being a smarty-pants. In fact, he was being…normal. I stood there, looking at him with his blue eyes sparkling through what appeared to be…tears?

"Eddie, I think we should be nice to everyone. I think there's good in everyone too; you just have to look a little harder in some than others." I loved repeating things my dad used to say.

"You must've had to look *really* hard in me," he said, like he was waiting for an answer and hopeful it, too, would be kind.

"Not really. I can tell a good heart, and you have a good heart, Eddie. I just know it," I said, almost convincing myself of it.

"You think so?" he asked.

"I know so."

Miss Thomas started social studies, and then we had science. Not a single time did Eddie bother me. In fact, it was so quiet behind me, I wasn't even sure he was there.

Just before the bell rang, Eddie got up to get the cleaner and the paper towels. I saw what he was doing, and I took the roll of paper towels from him, tore one off, and helped him clean his desk, just like I had promised.

"You sure are a good artist, Eddie."

And for the first time since I had known Eddie, I saw him smile. He had a dimple on each side of his face. And while his eyes still looked a little wild to me, he smiled a very nice smile. When the first bell rang, I had to leave. Eddie didn't leave until the second bell, so I looked at him and said, "See ya tomorrow!" And again, Eddie just looked stunned.

CHAPTER 7

The Calm Storm

Even Storm noticed a calmness about Eddie. We talked about it off and on Friday night. In fact, I think we were talking about it when we finally fell asleep a little after midnight. Storm asked me if I took in all stray animals. She laughed and reminded me of the day I walked over to her during PE and insisted that she play tag. "I didn't know what to think of you in that moment," Storm told me. "I felt all alone in a new school. I was scared to death, and there you were, insisting that I play."

"You're never alone, Storm. You know that, right?" I asked her.

"I know," she replied as she rolled over and said good night.

"Good night, Storm," I said as my eyes closed, and I drifted off to a dream I wished I could dream every night.

It was my dad, laughing hysterically—at what, I don't know. But there he was. It was so real; he looked so very real. He held his hands out to me. I was younger in my dream, but I ran and jumped into his arms. He held me so tight, and I held him too. I didn't want to let go, and I wasn't planning on it until, suddenly, he wasn't there any longer. My arms were wrapped around…absolutely nothing.

I woke up at that moment to find Storm sound asleep. The clock said 1:37 a.m., so I hadn't been asleep very long. And now I was wide awake, thinking about Dad and wishing he was still with us. He would know what to do about Henry. He would know where to take him and how to help him. He was so smart about everything: school, cars, building things, making us laugh, the list goes on and on. I was sad for a few minutes. But then that feeling just left, and I was happy—happy for Daddy because he got to be with Jesus every single day. How could I wish he was here when I knew how happy he must be now that his life is with Jesus? I had to go back to what Mom said because I know that it's true. I *will* see him again one day, and then we'll both get to spend every day with Jesus.

Those thoughts helped me get back to sleep. And while I tried really hard to dream about Daddy again, I didn't.

The next morning, Storm's dad had gone out and bought us doughnuts for breakfast. I had a chocolate-iced one, my favorite, and Storm ate one with sprinkles. I gathered all my stuff while Storm got ready for dance. I was going to see Storm dance today for the first time in several months, and then her parents were going to take me home afterward.

Storm looked like some kind of princess. She had on a white leotard, pink shoes, a pink tutu, and her hair was up on top of her head in a bun with some sort of white garland thing around her head. She looked like a completely different person! I stood there, looking at her, wondering what on earth she would ever have to worry about. She's smart; she's pretty; her parents are nice; she has a nice home. But I knew how anxious Storm gets sometimes. I had a whole slew of funny words and ways to distract her when I can tell she's getting worked up. I guess we all have problems; they just look different from one person to the next.

We walked into the dance studio, and Storm said, "I'll see you in a little bit. I have to go do my warm-ups." Her parents walked with me over to the seating area. I guess they had to do their warm-ups in some other room because I didn't see Storm again for about thirty minutes. Finally, eight girls entered the room. Storm was the tallest in the group. The instructor started the music, and the girls began to move all around the room. I watched Storm, but I don't think she ever knew where I was even sitting. It was like she was in a whole different world, dancing and being free. She moved with such grace and balance, at times standing on her toes in a way that almost made my feet hurt. I just watched my friend, every move that she made, and wished that she felt that free all the time. She looked as if she didn't have a worry in the world and that she was in complete control of everything. If only that could last for her outside of this room.

"You looked great out there!" I told Storm when she walked over to her parents and me.

"You really think so?" she asked.

"Yes, I really think so! You're very talented," I told her.

Storm made a funny face and replied, "I bet you say that to all your stray animals."

We laughed as we walked side by side to the car. We played rock paper scissors all the way to my house. "I wish I didn't have to go, but I know I have chores to do since it's Saturday."

"It's okay. I have to clean my room today too, and I have some math homework to finish," Storm said as she grabbed my overnight bag for me. "See you Monday!"

"See you then," I replied.

Henry had spent the night with a friend last night too, and he wasn't home yet. I wondered what Mom did while we were both gone. I bet she was lonely. I bet she watched some sad movie and ate a pint of ice cream. Had I known Henry was gonna be gone, Storm could've come over to our house. I should have thought of that sooner.

"Hey, Mom! How are you?" I yelled as soon as I entered through the front door.

"I'm fine. Did you have fun at Storm's?" she asked.

"Yes, you wouldn't believe what a great dancer she is, Mom! She is so good!" I informed her.

"That's great, Mabel. Is that something you'd be interested in doing?" she asked.

"No. That's not my talent at all. I'm not sure what my talent is, but it's certainly not ballet," I said, knowing full well that my dancing would be hazardous to my health and to everyone around me.

"Well, we all have talents, and if we don't use them, we lose them," Mom stated with much certainty.

"Maybe my talent is helping people," I proposed, just to see if Mom thought that was actually a talent.

"You know, Mabel, I think that is definitely one of your greatest talents. You do help people, and you make them feel good about themselves. Tim, I mean, Mr. Chapman told me about how you helped Eddie have a great day with the substitute teacher. That's almost a miracle from what I understand," she said with a little bit of a laugh.

I appreciated Mom seeing that as a talent, but I did catch the fact that she called my principal Tim and that he called her Maggie the other day. Why were they on a first-name basis all of a sudden? Were they friends now, and if so, when did that happen? I was just getting ready to ask something about that (I'm not sure what), but then suddenly, Henry raced through the front door and yelled something about not being stupid as he stomped up the stairs and locked himself in his bedroom.

"What on earth!" Mom exclaimed as she hurried up the stairs after him. "John Henry Thompson, you unlock this door right this instant," Mom said with authority. I heard the door unlock, but it didn't open. Quietly, I walked up the stairs and sat there, listening as Mom went into his bedroom and asked what was wrong. Henry was crying, and it was hard to put together what he was trying to say, but I think I got it. Apparently, his friend, William, the boy Henry had spent the night with, told Henry he was stupid because he couldn't read a menu. Henry made a joke of it when it happened, but I guess he had repeated it over and over in his head, and now he was upset about it all. He told Mom that it wasn't the first time somebody had made fun of him. He told her that kids were making fun of him in class and that Mrs. Jones even had to put one person out in the hallway for saying mean things to Henry.

Mom listened while Henry cried and tried to talk at the same time. It was obvious that my little brother was hurting, and that made me hurt too. I gathered my composure, stood up, and walked into Henry's room. I went over to his bed and just patted him on the shoulder. "I love you, Bubby," I said softly. "I love you just the way you are. You know why?" I asked. Henry didn't respond, but I could tell he was listening because his breathing slowed. "Well, I'll tell you why. Because God made you in His image, and God makes things beautiful." My Mom looked at me and touched my hand, squeezing it tightly. I continued, "You're gonna be okay, Henry. I promise you're gonna be okay."

Mom and I sat there with Henry until he fell asleep. He napped for a couple of hours and seemed to be much better when he woke up. We played a game of Monopoly, and Mom and I helped him read the cards. He actually ended up winning, which definitely made his day! And actually, the fact that he won and was so happy made my day too.

CHAPTER 8

The Sketch Pad

I decided that since I couldn't talk to my friends in class anyway, I would ask Michael if he would want to just keep our seating arrangement. Of course, Michael jumped at the chance to move. Eddie had either colored or cut every shirt Michael owned; he even cut Michael's hair on one occasion. Eddie was a lot calmer when I sat in front of him. He didn't write on me. He didn't cut my hair. He just sat there. I don't know if he was listening to the teacher or not, but he wasn't distracting anybody, which was a huge step for him.

Before the day was up, Mr. Foster let us have a little bit of free time in the room since it was raining outside. We got to get out some board games. Eddie started drawing on his desk again. I asked him to play Connect 4. We were gonna have like a tournament, but Eddie shook his head and continued to draw. I looked at his drawing, expecting to see fire-breathing dragons and torches and such. But this time, it was very different. It actually looked like the back of my head. Eddie had drawn the back of my head! He drew the backs of the two people to our left and the two people to our right with them sitting at their desks, and then he drew Mr.

Foster facing us with his hand pointing to something on the board. "You really are a talented artist, Eddie. You know, you gotta use it so you don't lose it." Eddie looked at me again and kind of smirked. There was just something about him. I couldn't put my finger on it, but I really did think that Eddie had a good heart. There was something very special about him. And although most people couldn't see it, I could, and that's why I wanted to keep sitting in front of him. If me sitting in front of him helped him to be still and listen, then that was exactly what I was gonna do. And believe it or not, Eddie had another really good day at school!

Henry's doctor appointment was tomorrow. When we talked about it at the dinner table, I asked to go. Mom quickly said, "No, Mabel, you have school tomorrow."

"But you and Dad always took us to our appointments. Now with Dad gone, I think I should be there to listen and ask questions," I argued.

"Mabel, you have school tomorrow," she repeated. "I think Henry and I can handle it."

I ran to Mom's office and got a blank sheet of paper. "Here," I said, handing her the blank piece of paper. "I want you to write everything down, okay? That way, you won't forget anything," I insisted.

"Yes, ma'am," Mom replied with a smile.

I was just worried about Henry. I couldn't stand to see him cry and to hear that kids were being mean to him. Nobody should ever be made to feel that way, especially my little brother. Henry asked a lot of questions about his doctor appointment. I think he was most afraid that he was gonna be getting some kind of shots. Mom assured him that he wouldn't.

Mom dropped me off at school the next morning. Mr. Chapman said hello to me when I got out of the car, but he didn't even ask why Henry wasn't getting out of the car. *Did he know where Mom and Henry were going today?* I wondered. *And if so, how did he know?* It was another example of just how strange adults are sometimes.

I walked into class with something in my backpack for Eddie. I had gotten a sketch pad a couple of years ago, and I never used it. Eddie wasn't there yet, so I dug it out of my book bag and placed it on his desk. He got there just as the bell rang. He came in, threw his book bag on his desk, and plopped down, being noisier than ever. Then, I think he saw the sketch pad but not before Mr. Foster asked him to enter class a little bit quieter, which seemed to set him off. He got settled and ended up having a pretty good day, but he was back to some of his old antics again, like stepping on people's shoes and making noises. He wasn't doing anything to me but to others around him. I turned around a couple of times, just as a reminder. Finally, when I saw Dylan drop his pencil and Eddie kick it halfway across the room, I turned around and whispered, "Draw something for me, Eddie. I brought you a sketch pad so you could use your talent. So draw something for me." That's all it took, and Eddie was quiet and calm. He had his math book out, but I wasn't sure if he was drawing or doing his math. I didn't really care as long as he wasn't getting into trouble.

At PE, I insisted to my friends that we let Eddie play war ball with us. Eddie came over and played. He was sure rough with the boys, but he wasn't with the girls, especially me. He had a gentle side, but something stirred in him, like a bunch of bees in a hive. When he got mad, he got mad quick, and that was just scary sometimes. Eddie had thrown his books clean across the room once in second grade. It scared everyone, including the teacher. He missed quite a bit of school after that. In fact, I don't remember seeing him again until third grade. Someone said he was homeschooled for a while, but I'm not certain of that.

I was worried about Henry and wondering how his doctor appointment was going. I guess I was more quiet than usual because on our way back from PE, Eddie asked me if I was okay. Can you believe that! Eddie Townsend asked someone if they were okay! I was right; he does have a good heart! I just told him that my brother was at the doctor and that I was worried about him. I didn't want to tell all my brother's business, but I did want to respond to Eddie in a way that said I appreciated him asking me if I was okay. He didn't say anything after that, and I wondered what he was thinking. At the end of the day though, when the bell rang, he leaned forward just before I stood up and said, "I hope your brother's okay." I turned around, smiled at Eddie, and headed toward the pick-up line.

When I got into the car, I just couldn't stand it any longer. "So what did the doctor say about Henry?"

Mom looked in the rearview mirror a brief moment before pulling away and said, "Well, they did a lot of tests today, and the doctor believes that Henry has something called dyslexia."

"Dyslexia? What is that?" I asked, not knowing if it was contagious or something serious.

"Well, Mabel, it's a learning problem that Henry's probably always had. It's just showing up now because he's trying to learn to read and write and do basic math," Mom said, as if her explanation was sufficient.

"So what's the plan? Is there some kind of medicine or something?"

"I've already spoken with Mrs. Jones and Tim… I mean Mr. Chapman."

There it is again… Tim. Makes no sense, I thought to myself.

"There is a teacher at school who has had special training in how to work with students who have dyslexia. Apparently, almost 20 percent of the population has dyslexia," Mom explained further.

"So he's not gonna die?" I asked, wanting to be certain.

"No, I'm not gonna die, Mabel. Well, I guess I will someday," my brother said with a smart-aleck tone.

I was definitely relieved to hear the news. Henry just has a reading problem, there's a teacher at school who can help him, and he's not gonna die from it. I recapped the conversation to make sure I didn't have any other questions. Henry seemed fine. Mom seemed relieved too. I guess we do all have our own problems. Henry's is dyslexia, Storm's is anxiety, and mine is Eddie! For some reason though, the thought of Eddie made me smile.

CHAPTER 9

Far, Far Away

Henry started being pulled out of class each day to work with Mrs. Conley, the teacher who knows how to help kids with dyslexia. For the next few months, I saw him about every day either walking past my room to see Mrs. Conley or walking back to his room after seeing her. He seemed a bit more confident these days, and at least he wasn't getting into trouble anymore. He finally started greeting Mr. Chapman again in the mornings at the drop-off line—Tim, as Mom calls him. That is just so funny!

There were only a couple of weeks left of fourth grade. Storm and I had continued our Friday night sleepovers. I still *loved* getting to have free day in PE, and Eddie had been on his best behavior. His artwork was so amazing! He drew a picture of Mr. Foster the other day with his glasses and wrinkles and even the mole just below his right eyebrow. It was obvious that Eddie was going to be a famous artist someday. He just needed the right tools.

I just so happened to be cleaning my room in preparation for Storm coming over, and I found some art pencils, specially just for sketching. I also found an eraser, a good one that looked like it had never been used. I thought I would surprise Eddie and get to school a little early just so I could put it in his desk. There is no telling what he would be able to draw if he had everything he needed—maybe the Empire State Building or some other skyscraper or maybe a field of flowers. No, on second thought, someone who draws fire-breathing dragons probably doesn't also draw pretty flowers, but you never know.

I got to school early and raced to class, placing the pencils and the eraser just inside his desk. He would see them the moment he sat down, and he would know they were from me. I got my notebook out and starting working on our morning work while I waited for the bell to ring and Eddie to arrive. Only Eddie didn't come to school. He wasn't there today; he didn't come the next day; and in fact, he missed the entire rest of the school year. *Where had he gone?* I wondered. *How could he leave without even saying goodbye, without saying goodbye to me?* It was the saddest I had been since my daddy's funeral. It felt just like someone had reached in and pulled off another piece of my heart, like it was taffy or something.

When I realized that Eddie wasn't coming back, I thought about all the conversations we had over the past few months: the ridiculous ones, the funny ones, and the serious ones. The one conversation that bothered me the most was the one about the scar on Eddie's face. It was a dandy, for sure. It started just to the left of his mouth and went high up on his cheek, close to the corner of his eye. I asked him one day when we were sitting on the playground, just the two of us, "How'd you get that scar?" I didn't want to be blunt like Henry is sometimes, so I made sure to sound like it wasn't anything out of the ordinary. He paused at first, like he didn't want to tell me, but then he explained that, one day, when he was at his babysitter's house, he was outside playing in a sandbox. His babysitter's dog, Milton, was outside too, keeping a close eye on Eddie. But another dog, a stray dog that was at least part pit bull, started growling at him and walking toward him from the corner of his street. Milton started barking and growling back, trying to scare the dog away, but there was no scaring him. Before Eddie could even think to run, the dog had bitten his tiny shoe off of his foot and came back once more, only to clamp down on the side of his face. He was only two years old, but he said he remembers everything about it, even being rushed to the hospital and having his face sewn up. He said he looked like a monster. And then he said that, sometimes, when he looks in the mirror, he still feels like he looks like a monster.

I could tell it was extremely hard for Eddie to tell that story, but I was glad that he trusted me enough to tell it. "It's not good to keep those things bottled up inside," I told him. So he described it in a way that made me visualize the entire horrific scene. While I was glad he shared such a difficult story, I could just kick myself for not saying more when he finished. I wanted to tell him that God was with him on that day when that mean old dog bit him. I wanted to tell him that he was beautiful just the way he was and that no mark on the outside should ever change what was on the inside. I wanted to tell him that I knew he liked me, and that I liked him too. But I didn't. I let time slip by, and I didn't tell him that I was glad we met and that I was glad I had him for a friend. Why did I let that happen! How could I have let that happen! And now, he's gone. He probably moved far, far away, and I'll never see him again. A big lump was in my throat now, and I had to do a lot of self-talk to keep from just bursting out crying right in the middle of science. I wiped away a few tears that streaked my face, mainly because I didn't want any of my classmates to know that I liked Eddie that way. I just wanted Eddie to know.

I suppose Mr. Foster knew how I felt because instead of moving Michael back over to the seat behind me, he moved Storm. It was good to have someone to talk to, even though we couldn't really talk much during class. I at least knew she was there. She even pretended to draw on the back of my shirt a couple of times just to try to make me smile and to let me know that she knew I was missing Eddie.

Just before school let out for summer break, Mrs. Lamkey came to our classroom door and asked Mr. Foster if she could speak with me for just a moment. Oh, how I missed her! She was so much fun; I think mainly because she liked writing as much as I do. Mr. Foster was nice enough, and I guess he did know me too, just in a different sort of way. He knew that I would be good for Eddie, but what he didn't know was that Eddie would be good for me. Eddie taught me about grace, tolerance, understanding, and forgiveness, things I had only heard about in Sunday school, but I'd never really had to put into practice.

I went to the door, and Mrs. Lamkey gave me a big hug. "How did she know I needed that?" I wondered. Without hesitation, Mrs. Lamkey said, "Mabel, I want to ask you something. Now you feel free to say no, and I promise it will be fine."

"Sure, Mrs. Lamkey. What is it?" I asked, wondering what in the world Mrs. Lamkey would ever need from me.

"I'm needing a helper during summer school, and Mr. Chapman said I could ask one really great student to help. Now I know your brother is going to be in my class for summer school, but I also know that the two of you get along really well."

"Yes, ma'am," I said proudly. "He's my only brother, and it's my job to look out for him."

"That is exactly what I thought you'd say. I know you would be giving up three weeks of your summer, but I also know that you love language arts. We'll be focusing on that and math during summer school. What do you think about helping me? I can even pay you to be my helper."

"Wow, Mrs. Lamkey! I'd be happy to help! You know I want to be a teacher someday, don't you?" I reminded her.

"I do, Mabel. I certainly do," she said with a smile. "And you'll make a great one. I just know it!" she said.

CHAPTER 10

Summer School

There was no break between the school year and summer school. I guess teachers didn't want kids to lose their momentum. After all, it *was* pretty great to get to sleep in and watch a little more TV than usual. So come Monday morning, Henry and I got up, just like we always did, and got ready for school.

I was a little nervous about it all. First, I was nervous because I wasn't entirely sure what Mrs. Lamkey was going to have me doing. Would I have my own group of students and be responsible for them learning? That seemed really scary to me. Maybe I would just grade papers and go around the room, helping kids when they needed it. I was also nervous about Henry. I know he has a really hard time with reading, writing, and math, and I just hate seeing him struggle like that, especially when he gets upset. The good news was that he had Mrs. Lamkey for summer school. She's the best writing teacher on the planet!

Mrs. Lamkey's approach to writing was telling kids to just get their thoughts and ideas down on paper. She would say, "Don't worry about spelling, don't worry about punctuation, don't worry about anything. Just picture it and then put it on paper however you'll be able to remember it. We can always go back and fix mistakes, but your thoughts are most important in writing," she said in such a way that it would make anyone want to try. Summer school was no different. On the very first day, she said something very similar to that.

I looked around the room and saw fear on kids' faces, but as soon as she said to relax, it was like letting air out of a big bunch of balloons—even Henry. He looked a little bit nervous but nothing like when we were trying to get him out of the car this morning. He kept saying pretty loudly, "I don't wanna go to summer school! I don't even like regular school!" Mom tried everything she could to coax him into getting out of the car, but nothing was working.

Finally, I took Henry's face and turned it toward mine. "Henry, Mrs. Lamkey is the kindest teacher. I know she can help you. You've just got to trust me," I pleaded. "Do you trust me, Henry?" I asked. "Do you trust me?"

"Yes, I trust you, Mabel," he said as he exhaled loudly, still not happy to be going to summer school.

"Besides," I told him, "I'm gonna be in the room with you the whole time. So if you need me, just holler. Well, don't holler," I corrected myself. "You know what I mean."

Mrs. Lamkey started with writing because she knew most of the kids in there needed a lot of help in that area. She wrote on the board, "My Special Place." She asked the students to write about their special place and that it could be anywhere. She reminded them to just get their thoughts on paper and that she didn't care if they misspelled every single word; she was just interested in their thoughts.

I looked over at Henry. His head was down, looking at his paper. After just a few seconds, he started writing…and writing…and writing. He looked just like I do when an idea pops into my head. When that happens, I can't think of or do anything else until I write it all down. That was Henry in this very moment.

Mrs. Lamkey asked me to walk around quietly and to only help if a student asked me for help. *I can do that,* I thought. *I'll just tiptoe around and see what they're coming up with.* I stayed away from Henry though because I didn't want to distract him in any way since he was on such a roll. I looked over kids' shoulders, and every now and then, I would whisper in their ear, "You can do it. Just think about a favorite place. There's no right or wrong because it's *your* favorite place."

Mrs. Lamkey believes in quiet writing time. Once started, kids have to be quiet, whether they're writing or not. Nearly thirty minutes had gone by, and not one student complained of a broken pencil lead or that they couldn't think of anything to write. They were all really into the assignment.

I noticed that Henry had stopped writing. He was holding his paper up and glaring at it. Thinking it would be a good time to check on him, I walked over and leaned down to read his paper.

I couldn't make much out of it. He had even spelled the title wrong, and Mrs. Lamkey had written that on the board. He looked up at me and asked what I thought. He seemed eager but also afraid to hear what I was going to say.

I knelt down beside Henry and said, "Okay, I think it's gonna be great. We just need to go through each line and get the spelling cleaned up a bit," I reassured him.

Honestly, I had no clue what his favorite place was, but I was most certainly going to figure it out. After we got the title corrected, I went to the first line, covering up all the words below it and around it so that he could focus on one word at a time. "What's this word?" I asked Henry.

"In," he said.

This could take a while, I thought to myself. We moved to the second word and then the third word, and before we got to the end of the line, I walked over to Mrs. Lamkey and asked if there was any way I could go out in the hallway and help Henry with his spelling. I held his paper up so that she could see what I was talking about.

"Yes, I think that would be a wonderful idea, Mabel," she agreed.

Henry moved his desk out into the hallway since he was already seated close to the door, and I grabbed an empty desk so that I wouldn't have to kneel down beside him. We worked and worked. I'd cover up his writing all but one word at a time, and he would tell me what it was. Then I would print it onto another piece of paper. I was absolutely amazed at the voice Henry had in his writing! What looked like some sort of word search puzzle had something very powerful inside. When we finished with the last word, I read the whole thing aloud…and cried, overjoyed with Henry's brilliant and creative thoughts that had been trapped and completely lost until today.

My Special Place
by John Henry Thompson

In my special place, I can soar with eagles, I can swim with the sharks, and I can feel the rubbery skin of dolphins.

In my special place, I can climb the tallest mountains, I can leap like a snow leopard, and I can feel the shape of the stars.

In my special place, I can ski the highest slope, I can ride the scariest roller coaster, and I can feel the biggest glacier.

In my special place, I can laugh at my daddy's knock-knock jokes, I can sit on his shoulders, and I can feel him kiss me on my forehead before he goes to bed.

Because my special place is in my mind.

I never looked at my brother the same way after that. I realized that he was amazing, he was never alone, he was strong, he was capable, he was always loved, he was created, he was victorious, he was chosen, he was beautiful, and he was most certainly enough in the eyes of Jesus and in the eyes of me, Mabel.

ABOUT THE AUTHOR

Janet Meeks has been a teacher, principal, school super-intendent, college professor, and mental health therapist. She lives with her husband in rural Kentucky, along with her cat, Margo. She has two grown children and loves spending time with them. In her free time, she also enjoys traveling with her husband and friends, visiting with family, eating out, watching movies, and listening to music.